God Owns— I Manage

A Handbook for
Managing God's Resources

by Michael D. McCann

STANDARD PUBLISHING
Cincinnati, Ohio 11-03018

Library of Congress Cataloging in Publication Data:

McCann, Michael D.
God owns—I manage: a handbook for managing God's resources / by Michael D. McCann.
p. cm.
ISBN 0-87403-668-2
1. Stewardship, Christian—Handbooks, manuals, etc. I. Title.
BV772.M387 1990
241'.68—dc20 89-49187
CIP

Sharing the thoughts of his own heart, the author may express views not entirely consistent with those of the publisher.

Contents

Introduction

God invites you to be His partner. More than that, He has *called* you to a partnership. If you are one of His people, you have already been enlisted for God's enterprise. You are a part of His mission in this world.

This is no ordinary partnership. Your Partner is no ordinary partner. He is the King of the universe. It is, of course, not an equal partnership. As owner, God provides all the resources, and it is His mission that the partnership is intended to fulfill. Your role is that of manager, using what He provides to participate in this purpose. How you use these resources is of immeasurable significance, affecting both time and eternity.

As you engage in this partnership, you will not be seeking your own benefit or advancement. Make no mistake—you *will* experience tremendous benefits from the partnership, but that is neither your focus nor your motivation. As God's partner, you will be pursuing His pleasure and honor and the advancement of His kingdom.

How does this partnership operate? What are the roles played by God and by you? What are the goals? What are the strategies? To answer these questions, let's back up and see how this partnership got started.

God established His kingdom on earth at creation. At first, there was perfect harmony in His kingdom as Adam and Eve lived in submissive fellowship with Him. Satan, however, led an invasion of God's kingdom. He introduced rebellion to God's planet, seducing Adam and Eve and establishing the kingdom of darkness. Ever since that time, he has been seeking to undermine God and overthrow His kingdom.

Today the battle continues. God's kingdom (comprising those who acknowledge Him as King, who worship and obey Him) is pitted against the kingdom of darkness (where Satan is in control). If Jesus is your Lord and Savior, then you are a part of God's kingdom. You are involved in this battle.

Of course, the outcome of this spiritual battle is already decided. Jesus won the decisive victory on the cross and in His subsequent resurrection. And a day is coming when God will call a halt to the war. His enemies will be defeated by a mere word from His mouth, and His kingdom will be completely and ultimately established. He will reign for ever and ever, He will abolish evil for eternity, and His foes will be punished and banished to Hell. God's people, however, will reign with Him forever. And God's kingdom will never be invaded again.

In the meantime, God has enlisted His kingdom people to be His partners. The mission is to exalt the King and to expand His kingdom. Nothing could be more significant, challenging, or rewarding.

What, then, are the roles of this partnership? God is King and owner of all. You, His servant, are a manager of a portion of His resources. He entrusts these resources to you (such as time, money, material goods, abilities—even your body and your relationships). And your task is to manage them according to His purposes. His priorities are to be your guide as you manage.

God owns; you manage. It's stated so simply. But it demands nothing less than all of you. It's a full-time vocation. It demands a one-hundred-percent effort. But when you get right down to it, isn't that what you want? What could be more fulfilling? You will be working together with the King of the universe in an enterprise that is bigger than life itself. You will be seeking to invest the life and resources God has supplied in the only venture that really counts. Would you want anything less?

Using This Handbook

This handbook is divided into two parts. Part one (Lessons 1-3) focuses on knowing our Partner. He is Creator, Owner, Lord, and Savior. As we come to know Him better, we will find greater motivation for managing effectively. we will find it more and more natural to think in terms of pleasing Him with our decisions about how we use His resources. The beginning place for proper management of our lives and resources is to know God.

Part two (Lessons 4-6) focuses on fulfilling our role as a manager. Since God is Creator, Owner, Lord, and Savior, He does not answer to us or anyone else. we answer to Him. We do what He wants. We manage His resources according to His desires. This part of the handbook will help you explore ways you can do just that.

This handbook combines insights with questions and activities to encourage you to investigate what the Bible teaches about managing God's resources and to apply what you learn to your life. Use it on your own in an individual study or as part of a group. Use it in a Sunday-school class or a Bible study. Use it with a discipleship partner, a friend, or your spouse.

If you use the handbook as part of a group, the leader will find the "Session Guide for Leaders" very helpful. This section is at the back of the book (page 45), and provides ideas for leading a group investigation of the truths of each lesson. Feel free to adapt each lesson to your group's own unique needs.

God Owns—I Manage. When we recognize the simple yet profound truth of that statement, we will find that we are truly in partnership with God.

Who Really Owns This Stuff?
Knowing God as Creator and Owner

This Land Is Whose Land?

After reading these words to this once popular song, discuss the questions that follow:

This land is your land, this land is my land,
From California to the New York island;
From the redwood forest, to the Gulf Stream waters,
This land was made for you and me.*

1. According to Psalm 24:1 and Colossians 1:16 and 17, how accurate is this song?

____

____

2. Is there a sense in which this song is correct? If so, in what sense?

____

____

3. What keeps people from recognizing that God is the owner of everything?

____

____

Getting Back to Basics

One of the most basic facts in Scripture is that God is the creator. Almost everything else is built upon this premise. Young children in Sunday school are taught this fact. But, by the time they become adults, they frequently lose the significance of this basic truth. Because God is the creator, everything belongs to Him.

Each of the passages below expresses this truth in some way. Choose one or both of the groups of passages below. Read the passages and summarize each one in eight words or less. (Try to avoid using the same summary for more than one passage.)

• *Group One*

Deuteronomy 10:14 ________________

____

1 Chronicles 29:11-14 ________________

____

• *Group Two*

Psalm 100:1-3 ________________

____

John 1:1-3 ________________

____

Psalm 50:10-12 ______________________

____

Romans 11:36 ______________________

____

Psalm 95:3-7 ______________________

____

1 Corinthians 8:6 ______________________

____

We cannot ignore the overwhelming testimony of the Bible regarding God's relationship to creation. Everything in the universe was made by Him (Genesis 1:1). Not only did He create everything, but He created it for himself (Colossians 1:16). For that reason, He and He alone has the right to claim ultimate ownership. We are only fooling ourselves when we think that what we have is ours. In fact, even when we give offerings to God, we are only giving back to Him what He already owns.

Questions to Consider

1. According to Psalm 100:1-3, which of the words below describe what God's ownership in our lives ought to bring? Circle all appropriate words:

Delight Drudgery Fear Anxiety Apathy Worship

Submission Anger Joy Rebellion Singing

2. Why should God's ownership of our lives logically lead to these responses?

____

____

3. Which of the words above describes the way you tend to respond to God's ownership in your life?

____

____

4. You may find that you do not always take delight in God's ownership in your life. Perhaps it is something with which you struggle frequently, or it may be only an occasional problem. Whenever you struggle with God's ownership of your life, how can you develop an appreciation for it?

____

____

____

Listing God's Assets

To say that God owns everything is a pretty general statement. We can repeat the words frequently without allowing them to sink in. List as many answers to the two questions on the next page as you can.

There may be some overlap in your responses to the questions. A few ideas are provided for each question.

1. What in this world does God own?	2. What in my life does God own?
—IBM	—my I.R.A.'s
—the mountains	—my schedule
______________________	______________________
______________________	______________________
______________________	______________________

What's Your Opinion?

Read each statement below. Determine your reaction to each and place a check (✓) in the corresponding column. (If you are using this material in a group, be ready to defend your answer.) Here is the code: **SA**=strongly agree; **MA**=mildly agree; **MD**=mildly disagree; **SD**=strongly disagree.

SA	MA	MD	SD	
__	__	__	__	1. Most Christians understand that God is the owner of everything in their lives.
__	__	__	__	2. Most Christians readily and consistently acknowledge God's ownership of their lives and all they possess.
__	__	__	__	3. Acknowledging God's ownership over all we are and possess brings a sense of joy and peace.
__	__	__	__	4. Our American concepts of self-sufficiency and private ownership hinder us from recognizing God's ownership in our lives.
__	__	__	__	5. If we took God's ownership seriously, our lives would be radically different.

Living Under God's Ownership

"Okay. So I accept God's ownership. The Bible teaches it. It makes sense. I have no problem acknowledging God as Creator and Owner. But how can I let that truth impact my daily life? What difference does it make?"

That is worth pursuing. The beginning point of managing God's resources is taking His ownership seriously. What will my life look like when I integrate this truth into my activities and relationships? Will I be required to sell all I have and give it to God? Do I have to renounce all desire for money or material objects? Must I feel guilty for buying things I don't need? Do I need to live such a radical life-style that my friends will avoid me like nuclear waste?

Perhaps the best way to wrestle with these and similar questions is to establish a few perspectives and disciplines. Below are three suggestions, with each one followed by some questions to help you clarify your thinking on the issues brought up in the suggestion. Read through them and choose one or more of the suggestions and put it into practice this week.

- **A Challenge**

A good place to begin is to challenge yourself to see everything you call your own as belonging to God. Begin each day by acknowledging that it is His day (Psalm 118:24) and should be lived according to His desires. Challenge yourself when you become possessive in your thinking. When you start becoming attached to things and thinking they belong to you, catch yourself and correct your false views.

Questions to Consider

1. How can you tell when you are becoming possessive of God's belongings? What indicators might tell you when this is happening? An example: I become extremely or unreasonably upset when something breaks.

2. What can you do to challenge yourself when you become possessive?

3. Is there any sense in which we can say to someone, "This is my house; . . . my car; . . . my [anything]"? If so, how? If not, why not?

- **A Prayer**

A second discipline to develop is to spend more time in prayer before making purchases. If it is God's money, you will want to use it as He desires. Although God will not likely tap you on the shoulder or send an angel with the answer, praying is indispensable in gaining His guidance and wisdom.

Questions to Consider

1. Name one item you wish you had not bought. Did you pray before you bought it? If so, do you think you misinterpreted the answer, or why do you now wish you had not bought the item? If you did not pray beforehand, how might prayer have influenced your decision?

2. Listed below are some suggested questions to ask as you prayerfully determine whether making a particular purchase is making the best use of God's money. What are some others you could ask?

"Is this something I can live without?"
"Why is this purchase important to me?"
"Can I purchase this without using credit?"

____

____

____

____

• **A Journal**

Keep a journal to evaluate how well you are progressing in acknowledging God's ownership. You can write in your journal daily or weekly, but you need to set some regular interval between writings. Ask yourself questions like the ones below to generate ideas for what to write in your journal.

1. What in my day (or week) indicates that I am seeing everything as belonging to God?
2. What actions reveal that I need to grow more in yielding ownership to God?
3. Am I clinging too much to certain material objects or to money? What does that reveal about my view of ownership?
4. What Scriptures have I read that remind me that my life and possessions really belong to God?

Getting Personal

What good is it to explore Biblical truths, such as God's creatorship and ownership, if we don't honestly examine our lives in relation to them? Frankly, it can do more harm than good. Such an approach develops a habit of hearing God's Word without obeying it. That is a hard habit to break once it gains momentum.

The truths of today's study hit hard. We do not belong to ourselves. Our possessions, as we like to think of them, really are not our possessions. We have them on loan. They belong to the Creator of all things. He has allowed us to enjoy them for a time, but we must always be ready to let them go.

Think honestly about your own life. Do you need to sharpen your focus on ownership? Put an "X" on the line somewhere between the two extremes to indicate where you are in your personal growth:

I constantly yield ownership to God	_______________________________	I am unwilling to yield ownership to God

Now Answer These Two Questions

1. What in my life is evidence that I am learning to yield ownership to God?

____

____

2. What in my life is evidence that I need to grow more in yielding ownership to God?

____

____

Scripture Memory Verse

Psalm 24:1 or Deuteronomy 10:14

For Further Reflection

Explore the implications of God's ownership more by completing this activity:

Contrast a Christian who daily acknowledges God's ownership in all his life with a Christian who thinks he owns his life and possessions. (Consider: what does each value most? What goals might each pursue? How does each view his time, abilities, job, family, money, possessions, future? What would bring joy to each? What would bring anger?)

List your ideas below:

A Christian who daily acknowledges God's ownership in all his life.	A Christian who thinks he owns his life and possessions.
______________________	______________________
______________________	______________________
______________________	______________________
______________________	______________________

Lesson Two

Who Calls the Shots?

Knowing Jesus as Lord

Getting Started

Read the two statements below. Then respond to the discussion questions:

A. Jesus is Lord.

B. Jesus is Savior.

Questions to Consider

1. Which truth above demands more from us? Why?

____

____

2. Which truth do you think is more popular with Christians in society? Why?

____

____

Lordship and Obedience

The previous lesson focused on God as our creator and owner. It was designed to help you explore the fact that everything and everyone belongs to God since He is the creator of all. No one can say, "My life is my own." Everyone is indebted to God for his or her life and for everything he or she possesses.

This study picks up where the previous one left off. The focus of this entire series is that God is working with us to accomplish His purposes in this world. In a sense, we are involved in a partnership with God. To participate in this partnership effectively, we must understand who God is and who we are in relation to Him. He is the creator and the owner. Because of this, He is Lord. He rules all creation. All authority belongs to Him. Although He delegates authority to kings and rulers, church leaders, parents, and husbands, all authority is ultimately His. He is sovereign and answers to no one. In fact, everyone that has ever lived will have to answer to Him when Jesus returns. Imagine all the most powerful authorities you can think of (Caesar, Napoleon, Hitler, Lenin, Stalin)—they will all have to give an account to Jesus.

This study will focus upon Jesus as our Lord.

Convince Me!

Imagine that a Christian has just said to you that he isn't concerned about obeying Jesus. He just enjoys the privileges he has as a Christian and lives to enjoy himself. If it feels good to obey what Jesus has said, he does it. But he doesn't make a big deal of it. Choose at least one of the following groups of verses to develop a convincing argument for why he needs to be concerned about total obedience to Jesus.

• *Group One*

Matthew 7:21-29; 28:18; Luke 17:7-10; Romans 14:7-10

____

____

____

• *Group Two*

Luke 6:46-49; 17:7-10; Colossians 1:15-18; Revelation 17:14

____

____

____

• *Group Three*

Luke 17:7-10; 2 Corinthians 5:9, 10; Philippians 2:5-11; Colossians 3:23-25

____

____

____

Lord and Savior

A balanced view of Jesus sees Him as both Lord and Savior. We will explore the *Savior* aspect of His nature in the next lesson, but the beginning place in relating to Jesus is to approach Him as the *Lord*. We must understand that He is the Sovereign Ruler of the universe, the King, the Ultimate Authority! Then we can consider how He is—or can be—our Savior.

There are two reasons that we must relate to Jesus as Lord before we can relate to Him as Savior. First, He was Lord before He was Savior. His role as Lord is based on who He is and always has been. His role as Savior is based on something He did at a certain point in time: He died to save us. So, while His role as Savior is of incredible importance, He would still be Lord even if He were not Savior. Even if He never died to save anyone, we would still be obliged to obey Him as Lord. Thus—and this is the second reason His lordship precedes His role as Savior—His lordship is universal, but His role as Savior is limited. That is not to say there are those who cannot be saved by Jesus, or that some might be saved by another savior. It simply recognizes that not everyone will be saved; not everyone will receive His salvation. But someday everyone will acknowledge His lordship (Romans 14:11).

The Scriptures indicate that Jesus has total authority. The universe is subject to His will. Although He allows much freedom at the present, He will ultimately call all people to give an account for everything they have done in relation to His commands. At that point, they will all worship and submit to Him (Philippians 2:9-11). And they will have no choice but to accept His assignment for their final and eternal destiny.

Jesus expects total obedience to Him. And why not? He rules. He calls the shots. Our basic relationship to Him is that He is our Master and we are His slaves. For the believer, the relationship is much more than that, but that is the basic context for every other kind of relationship we have with Jesus—friend, beloved, brother, sister, to name just a few. Salvation is not available to those who will not bend the knee in submission to Jesus. We cannot receive a half Jesus. We must accept Him as Lord and Savior.

Jesus Is Lord: An Overview

Look up the Scriptures cited below. Then write four headings to complete the following outline that describes Jesus' lordship. When you have finished writing your headings, read the paragraphs that follow the outline. They provide some commentary on the verses cited and may help you clarify the ideas you developed as you read the Scriptures. Remember, read the Scriptures on your own first and decide how you think you would label the four areas; then read the commentary to see how your ideas compare with those presented there.

Jesus Is Lord

A.____ (Colossians 1:15-18)

B. ____ (Philippians 2:5-11)

C. ___________________________Romans 14:7-12; 2 Corinthians 5:9, 10)

D. ____(Colossians 3:17)

The lordship of Jesus has been presented in terms that sound strange to twentieth-century American ears. We are not used to thinking in terms of absolute rule and authority. But Jesus is not Lord because He was elected by a popular majority. He is Lord because He is God.

In Colossians 1:15-18, we see He is **Lord in creation**. To be the "firstborn over all creation" does not mean He was the first one created. He could not be "over all creation" if He himself were part of creation. *Firstborn* indicates preeminence or authority. Paul makes it clear: "all things were created by him and for him" (Colossians 1:16). Thus, He is still involved in His creation. He did not simply create everything and let it go. After all, He created it for himself, so He has a vested interest in it. "In him all things hold together" (Colossians 1:17). He will not let His creation fall apart. He holds it together so it can serve Him in the way He intends for it to.

It is through the church that His lordship over His creation is to be demonstrated to creation. The church consists of those who recognize His lordship. "He is the head of . . . the church" (Colossians 1:18) because He is the head of all creation. Christians do not "make" Him Lord, although we often use that terminology. In fact, He is already Lord; we simply need to recognize that fact.

The resurrection is the central fact in the church's faith in her Lord. The Lord of the church is **Lord in resurrection**. It was in this act that he proved He was indeed the Creator, the author of life. As Paul explains in Philippians 2:5-11, God exalted Him; He proved He was Lord. Because of that action, God now demands that every knee shall bow and every tongue confess that Jesus Christ is Lord.

Because of the resurrection, then, we can recognize that Jesus is Lord. If we fail to do so in this life, we will recognize Him as **Lord in judgment**. Romans 14:7-12 sounds very much like the passage in Philippians as it quotes Isaiah 45:23: "Every knee shall bow before me; every tongue will confess. . . ." Here, however, the context is the judgment. "So then, each of us will give an account of himself to God" (Romans 14:12). It is clear that Jesus will be God's agent in judgment just as He was the agent of creation. Paul writes in 2 Corinthians 5:9 and 10 that "we must all appear before the judgment seat of Christ."

From the beginning, then, Jesus has been Lord. He was Lord in creation. He was Lord in resurrection. And He will be Lord in judgment. And He must be **Lord in our lives** as well. We must recognize His lordship and live our lives accordingly. Paul explains how in Colossians 3:17. "Whatever you do, whether in word or deed, do it all in the name of the Lord Jesus."

"Whatever you do," Paul says. Jesus is Lord of all. We cannot divide our lives into religious and secular, and recognize His lordship only over the religious. He is Lord of the secular, too. He is Lord of "whatever."

The Meaning of Lordship

Second Corinthians 5:9 summarizes what our response should be to Jesus as our Lord: "We make it our goal to please Him." God does not exist to please us; we exist to please and glorify Him. He is the potter; we are the clay. We are to be what He wants us to be.

Read the excerpt below from *Call to Discipleship,** by Juan Carlos Ortiz (pp. 46-49).

In Jesus' parable of the servant, He tells us that all our time is His. The eight hours we work, the eight hours we sleep, and the other eight hours also are His. Perhaps after we return home from our job we say, "Tonight I'll take a shower, look at television for a bit, and then go to bed. The pastor told me there would be a meeting tonight, but I deserve a rest. It's enough that I attend a church meeting once a week. I deserve. . . ."

You deserve what, Mr. Slave? We deserve nothing because we are servants. We were bought by Jesus Christ. All our hours belong to Him. The servant in Jesus' parable, while he was out in the field, was not thinking, "I'll take a shower when I get home, and then have a nice snack." No, he was thinking, "What shall I prepare for my master?" While he was plowing he thought, "Shall I fix him rice and beans? No, he had that yesterday. A steak with french fried potatoes? No, he doesn't like fried potatoes too much. Better baked potatoes." He was thinking of the master, not of himself.

We are more like the man who comes in from work and asks his wife, "Who's going to preach at church tonight?"

"Juan Carlos, I think."

"Ahh, then I needn't go."

But even if he did go the choir would have to sing nice . . . and the meeting not be too long. We see ourselves as the lords who sit in the pews and Jesus as our servant. We are all upside down. We say "Lord" with our mouth but by our attitude we call Him slave. "Lord, I'm going out in the car. Please drive the car. Don't let us crash."

"Lord, my husband needs a better job because he's not earning enough."

"Yes, madam."

"Oh, help my child, he has examinations today. Please help, Lord. . . ."

Lord? Or servant? We should say "Lord" only when we are ready to give ourselves to Him and be His slaves. "Come on," He says, "prepare something for me to eat and properly clothe yourself and serve me until I have eaten and drunk and *afterward* you will eat and drink."

We cannot serve Jesus if we don't give ourselves as His servants. The satisfaction of the servant is to see the Lord satisfied.

Jesus ends His story by saying, "Does the master thank the slave because he did the things which were commanded of him?" No, says Jesus. We don't need to be thanked for the things we do. "So you too, when you do all the things which are commanded, can only say, 'We are unworthy slaves. We have done only that which we ought to have done.'" Can anyone say, "I have done everything that God commanded?" If that is so, we are ready for a graduation ceremony. When a person does everything the Lord commands, He gives him a diploma. And the diploma reads: *unprofitable servant.*

Once I heard the announcer in a meeting introduce the preacher saying, "And now, the great servant of God." The organ played and the spotlights focused as the "great servant" appeared. But if he is great, he is not a servant. And if he is a servant, he is not great. "Come, gird thyself and serve me until I have eaten and drunk and after that ye shall eat and drink." Our eating will be in heaven. And here on earth our eating and our refreshment and our joy will be when we see Jesus satisfied with our work for Him. He is the Lord, and we are His servants.

Your Reaction

Use the questions on the next page to express your reaction to the comments above.

**Call to Discipleship,* Juan Carlos Ortiz, ©1975 by Bridge Publishing, Inc., South Plainfield, NJ. Used by permission.

1. With what statement or concept do you agree most? Why?

____

____

2. With what do you most disagree? Why?

____

____

3. How do Ortiz's comments relate to the Scriptures you have studied in this lesson?

____

____

Jesus Is Lord: So What?

Clichés lose their impact. They become trivial. We cease to think about their significance. Unfortunately, the truth that *Jesus is Lord* has become little more than a cliché for many who consider themselves to be Christians. But think about it. If Jesus calls the shots in the universe, if He is in control of life, if He is returning to judge the living and the dead, if I will someday have to give an account for everything I have done, then *Jesus' lordship is anything but trivial!*

We need to integrate into our daily thinking the concept that we are here to please the Lord Jesus. We exist for His satisfaction. We begin to place ourselves under Jesus' authority when we seek to know what He wants us to do and then attempt to do it—without grumbling, without arguing. Submitting to Jesus' lordship means we delight in obeying Him. (See Psalm 40:8.)

How can you develop a life-style of submission to Jesus? A complete and adequate answer is more involved than can be considered in one sitting. But here are a few suggestions to assist you in your desire to live under His authority.

•A Question to Ask

Try asking this question throughout each day: *"What does Lord Jesus want me to do?"* When you are in a conversation, or driving your car, or busy at work, or in the middle of a conflict, or deciding what to eat, or choosing how to use your free time, or playing ball, learn to ask that question. Try to think about the Lord's values, priorities, and ethical standards. (By the way, the answer to that question will not always look "religious." It may involve something as unreligious as taking a nap. Or it may be something that does not seem like the "nice" thing to do, like confronting someone who is engaged in sin.)

Don't be discouraged if you do not always feel certain about the answer. Sometimes, pleasing Jesus is more a matter of asking the right question than having the right answer. God is more concerned with developing us into submissive servants (who don't always have it all figured out) than He is in making us spiritual eggheads who always have all the answers.

Questions to Consider

1. In which part of your life do you most regularly need to ask, "What does Lord Jesus want me to do?" Choose one of the suggestions below.

____When I'm at work
____When I'm driving
____When I'm in conversation
____When I'm choosing a television program
____When I'm thinking of purchasing something
____When I don't get what I want
____When I've been rejected by someone
____When I'm at home with my family
____When I'm around an attractive person of the opposite sex
____When I have free time
____When I'm with my friends

2. Consider the area you chose above. What might be different in your life if you asked the suggested question in that situation?

____

____

•Some Thoughts for Meditation

Meditate on these three truths:
God knows what is best for my life.
God wants what is best for my life.
God has the power to give what is best for my life.

Questions to Consider

1. How can meditating on these truths help you give Jesus more control of your life?

____

____

2. On a scale of 1 (not at all) to 10 (completely, without a shadow of a doubt), how much do you really believe these three truths?

1 2 3 4 5 6 7 8 9 10

3. What evidence of your belief can be seen in the way you live?

____

____

Responding to Jesus as Lord

In light of the truths you have studied and absorbed today, personalize your response to the Lord Jesus by completing these sentences as they reflect your thoughts and intentions:

1. When I think of Jesus' lordship, I. . . .

____

____

____

2. Because Jesus is Lord, and has all authority in Heaven and on earth, I submit these areas of my life to Him:

____

____

Scripture Memory Verse

Matthew 28:18 or Romans 14:7, 8

For Further Reflection

To expand upon this lesson, explore the concept of Jesus' lordship in more depth. Look up each passage below and jot your answer to this question: "What does this passage reveal about the Lord?" (By the way, Scripture refers to Jesus as *Lord* much more frequently than as *Savior*.)

What does each of the following passages reveal about the Lord?

Psalm 29:1-11 ______________________________

____

Psalm 93:1, 2 ______________________________

____

Psalm 96:4-13 ______________________________

____

Psalm 99:1-5 ______________________________

____

Psalm 103:19 ______________________________

____

Psalm 111:10 ______________________________

____

Psalm 113:4, 5 ______________________________

____

Psalm 115:3 ______________________________

____

Psalm 118:1 ______________________________

____

Psalm 135:5, 6, 13 ____

Psalm 145:1-3, 8-13

Psalm 147:5, 6

Matthew 7:29

Matthew 9:6

Matthew 28:18

Now, in the space below, write a prayer to God praising Him for His lordship and reign, and submitting your total self to Him.

Overwhelmed by Grace

Knowing Jesus as Savior

So Great a Salvation

Jesus is our Savior. He brings salvation from the past, in the present, and for the future. But did you ever stop and think of all that Jesus saves us from?

A number of Scriptures could be cited to produce a list of things from which Jesus saves us. Consider but a few: Romans 8:18-25; Philippians 3:20, 21; 2 Peter 3:8-14; Revelation 20:11—22:21. These passages reveal that when Jesus returns, some pretty awesome events will occur. The universe (heavens and earth) will be destroyed by fire, and God will create a new order of things (2 Peter 3:8-14). Our old, decaying (or decayed) bodies will be changed and replaced with new ones that will resemble Jesus' perfect resurrection body (Philippians 3:20, 21). We will live with Jesus in the New Jerusalem, free of decay and disintegration. The old order will have passed away, along with its sin, sickness, pain, sorrow, and crying. The curse that resulted from sin in the Garden of Eden will be abolished. And God's people will see Him face to face. We will reign with Him forever and ever (Revelation 20:11—22:21).

Below is a partial list of items Jesus saves us from—based on the passages cited above and others. Some of these are occurring right now. Some of them will not be realized until Jesus returns and we live with Him forever. Some of them occur partially now and will be fully experienced with Jesus in eternity.

From What Does Jesus Save Us?

Sin
God's wrath
Separation from God
Physical death
Spiritual death
Eternal death
Our sinful condition/corruption
Our sinful world
Satan and demons
Injustice
Decay
Sickness
Weeds/thistles
Weariness/fatigue
Defects
Meaninglessness
Emotional disorders
Conflict/broken relationships
Poverty
Hunger
Slavery/oppression

1. Put a check (✓) beside any of the above you hadn't ever related Jesus' salvation to before.

2. Which three items do you sense the greatest need for Jesus to save you from? Put an upward arrow (↑) beside them.

3. Add anything else to the list that you think belongs there from a Biblical perspective.

____

____

____

____

We Need a Savior

God is Creator and Owner of the universe. He is Lord (ultimate authority) of all. He has the right to do whatever He pleases. No one can command Him. He does only as He wills. He owes us nothing; we owe Him everything. He could command us and punish our disobedience, and the situation would be fair.

We can thank God that what He chooses is not evil, but is good and right. He is not a merciless ogre who daily plans our misery. He has issued commands and laws, but they are only for our own good. They are righteous because God is righteous. Nevertheless, because God is righteous, He must punish our disobedience to His commands. The penalty for sin is eternal separation from God in Hell. That is not desirable, but it is just. God could have left it at that, and we would all go to Hell because we have all disobeyed God (Romans 3:23). But God, in His infinite mercy, love, and wisdom, devised a way for Him to be just and still give sinners His eternal riches, not His eternal wrath. This is salvation.

Read and study Titus 3:3-8 and Ephesians 2:1-10. Then answer the accompanying questions. Discuss them with someone else who has studied these passages.

- **Titus 3:3-8**

1. How does verse 3 describe our condition before we came to Christ?

____

2. What was God's attitude toward us while we were in that condition (verse 4)?

____

3. What did God do for us while we were in that condition (verses 5-7)?

____

____

4. How are we to respond to God's mercy and grace (verse 8)?

____

____

- **Ephesians 2:1-10**

1. How do verses 1-3 describe our condition before we came to Christ?

____

2. What was God's attitude toward us while we were in that condition (verses 4-7)?

____

3. What did God do for us (verses 4-9)?

____

____

4. What is responsible for our salvation? What is not responsible (verses 8, 9)?

____

____

5. How are we to respond to our salvation (verse 10)?

____

____

Salvation in a Nutshell

The message of the Bible is that the Creator-King has reached down to His rebellious creatures (humans) and made a way for them to be saved. This emphasis is beautifully explained in Ephesians 2:1-10 and Titus 3:3-8.

Our Former Condition

Before we came to Christ for salvation we were. . . .

- *Dead.* "As for you, you were dead in your transgressions and sins" (Ephesians 2:1). When Adam and Eve sinned in the Garden of Eden, the element of physical death entered the world. We have all inherited this consequence of Adam's sin: our bodies are decaying and will die.

  We experience spiritual death, however, as a result of our own sin, not Adam's (Ezekiel 18:20). Spiritual death results when one's spirit is separated from God, who is the source of life. Sin brings that separation. Unless we are rescued from spiritual death and raised to life, we will suffer the eternal consequence of spiritual death: eternal separation from the presence of God, eternal "death" in Hell.

- *Dominated.* Sin is addictive. The more we sin, the more sin controls us. Because of our sinful condition, we have become dominated by the world system, the devil ("the ruler of the kingdom of the air"), and the flesh (rendered "sinful nature" in the NIV; Ephesians 2:2, 3). Titus 3:3 echoes this principle: "We too were foolish, disobedient, deceived and enslaved by all kinds of passions and pleasures."

- *Damned.* The just result of our sin is that we are placed under God's holy wrath. His wrath will be expressed toward unforgiven sinners when He returns to judge the living and the dead. Those whose sins have not been forgiven will be assigned to live (exist) forever in Hell with unending punishment.

Our Savior's Solution

God could have let us continue in our desperate condition and receive our punishment. That would have been fair. But God is more than fair—more than just—He is also loving; He is gracious. And He yearns to see everyone freed from the penalty of sin.

- *His solution is based on His nature.* God's holiness requires Him to punish sin. If He remained indifferent to sin and injustice, He would not be good; He would not be holy. But because He is loving as well as holy, He desires what is best for us. He is merciful and takes pity on our doomed condition (Ephesians 2:4; Titus 3:5). Being kind, He wants to deal with us tenderly (Ephesians 2:7; Titus 3:4).

• *His solution is called "grace."* Grace means that we receive God's love and acceptance even though we do not deserve it. And it is only by grace that we can be saved (Ephesians 2:8; Titus 3:7). We get God's best when we deserve the worst. We receive Heaven when we deserve Hell. The basis for this grace is in Jesus Christ. He was treated as we deserve to be treated (taking the wrath of God on the cross) so that we could be treated as He deserves to be treated (receiving God's riches in Heaven).

The means of receiving God's grace is faith—taking God at His word (Ephesians 2:8). Our own good works contribute nothing—absolutely nothing—to our salvation (Ephesians 2:9). Jesus' good work on the cross has paid the price one hundred percent. Salvation is a free gift for those with faith.

Our Present Situation

Receiving God's grace creates a whole new situation for us. It is, in fact, a whole new life! The helpless, hopeless condition we created for ourselves is totally erased and replaced with a situation we could never have expected apart from God's mercy toward us.

• *We are saved from God's wrath* (Ephesians 2:8-10; Titus 3:8). Salvation from wrath is only a part of the total package of salvation, but it may well be the most significant one. Ultimately, we will be saved from all the consequences of sin. (See the list at the beginning of this lesson.)

• *We are God's workmanship* (Ephesians 2:10). When we enter a saving relationship with God through Jesus, He enters our life through the Holy Spirit (Titus 3:6) and begins a major reconstruction project. He begins a process of recreating us to be more like Jesus, a process that continues throughout our lives (Philippians 1:6). This restructuring of our inner selves enables us to do good works—not works that save us, but works that express our gratitude for our salvation. Although our good works do nothing to save us, they are the natural and necessary result of our being saved.

This truth has profound implications for living as a manager of God's resources. In the remaining lessons, we will explore *how* to manage those resources, but this truth is at the heart of *why* we do so. Knowing we have received, and continue to receive, God's grace drives us. Knowing we belong in Hell but will, instead, live forever in Heaven motivates us to do all we can to please our Savior. We will not always live up to this ideal, but failure to attempt it reflects a serious lacking in the person's faith—perhaps he has never really believed on the Lord at all. Saving faith is a grateful faith that desires to express love to the Savior for His awesome mercy.

Summarizing the Gospel

Suppose a nonbeliever is interested in learning about your faith and asks you the questions below. Based on your study of the passages above, how would you answer his questions?

1. Why do we need to be saved?

____

2. What has God done to provide for our salvation?

____

____

3. How can we be saved?

4. How should we respond to God for saving us?

Jesus Is Savior: So What?

When Jesus enters our lives as Savior, we can expect to see changes. They may not be dramatic (although for some they are), but they are real. They may be gradual and not immediately detected. But if anyone is in Christ, he is a new person (2 Corinthians 5:17). What difference does it make to know Jesus as Savior?

- **Assurance**

Accepting Jesus as Savior gives us assurance. If it were possible to be saved by works, one would always wonder whether he had done enough, whether his good deeds exceeded his sins. But with Jesus as Savior, we can know we are saved. God has promised eternal life through Him (1 John 5:10-13), and He cannot lie. We can know for certain we are bound for Heaven.

Questions to Consider

1. What would you expect to observe in a person who is certain of his salvation?

2. How certain are you of your salvation?

3. If you are certain of your salvation, what makes you certain?

4. If you are uncertain of your salvation, what is causing your uncertainty? How can you become certain? (See Mark 16:16; Acts 2:38; 16:31; Romans 10:9, 10; Galatians 2:16; Ephesians 2:8-10.)

• **Gratitude**

When a person is saved, he is filled with gratitude to God. He knows his salvation could not be earned, but only received as a gift. For that gift he is grateful. It is not always obvious, but it is present.

Questions to Consider

1. Do you agree or disagree with the following statement? "God cannot save a person who has no gratitude for His saving grace." Support your position.

___

___

2. What evidence would demonstrate that a person has gratitude to God for salvation?

___

___

• **Obedience**

Knowing Jesus as Savior brings a right approach to obedience, to doing good works. We seek to obey more than ever, but not to earn salvation; that would be impossible. Instead, we obey in order to express our love to our Savior. Our delight in obeying Jesus increases because He has now accepted us—even though we do not deserve it.

Questions to Consider

1. What would indicate a person is doing good works to try to earn his salvation? What thoughts might such a person have while doing good works?

___

___

2. What would indicate a person is doing good works to express love and gratitude for the Savior? What thoughts might such a person have while doing good works?

___

___

My Prayer of Gratitude

A look at our sinful rebellion against a good and perfect Lord ought to bring remorse. God poured out kindness on us by providing us with food, shelter, sustenance, sunshine and rain, and a beautiful creation to savor with our senses. He wanted us to fill our lives with goodness, but we rejected Him. We considered His involvement in our lives an intrusion. So we spit in His face and told Him He was not welcome.

How foolish! We rejected the Bread of Life to scavenge among the garbage cans of sin. And we continued in that way, refusing to admit that God was right and we were wrong. We would not admit God's profound goodness and our own stupid rebellion. How offensive! How deserving of punishment! And yet, rather than punish, God saved us.

A look at God's gracious and merciful salvation ought to bring deep gratitude and love. Anyone with true, saving faith can see that his only legitimate response to God's grace (acceptance though we deserve His wrath) can be a life of obedience and submission to God, a desire to please Him with good works. These good works are not offered to earn salvation. We have already received salvation as a gift. Rather, they are the heartfelt response of humble, saving faith. As Paul wrote in Romans 12:1 and 2:

> Therefore, I urge you, brothers, *in view of God's mercy*, to offer your bodies as living sacrifices, holy and pleasing to God—this is your spiritual act of worship. Do not conform any longer to the pattern of this world, but be transformed by the renewing of your mind. Then you will be able to test and approve what God's will is—His good, pleasing and perfect will.

Below, express your gratitude to Jesus in your own words as a prayer of thanksgiving and commitment.

Jesus, I thank you. . . .

____

____

____

____

I want to demonstrate my gratitude to You by. . . .

____

____

____

____

Memory Verse

John 3:16 or Ephesians 2:8-10

For Further Reflection

Ephesians 2:1-10 provides a picture of a Christian before and after coming to Christ. Reread this passage and write your own "Ephesians 2 Testimony" by completing the thoughts suggested below.

My Ephesians 2 Testimony

What I was like before I trusted Jesus for salvation (attitudes, values, habits, motives, etc.):

____

____

How I came to recognize my need for Jesus:

Promises of God I am now claiming by faith:

Changes in my life since I received Christ:

Good works I am now doing or preparing to do:

So What?

Our Response to Our Creator, Owner, Lord, and Savior: Management

Entrusting Your Resources to Others

Below are several examples of possessions we entrust to others. Look at each example and answer this question: "What do you expect from those to whom you have entrusted it/them?" Write your answer(s) in the appropriate column.

What Is Entrusted	To Whom It Is Entrusted	What You Expect
Children	Baby-sitter	
Money	Bank	
Car	Mechanic	
Health	Doctor	

A Parable

Jesus is Creator and Owner. He is Lord and Savior. All we have belongs to Him and is merely entrusted to us. So how are we to respond to Him? What does He want us to do with His possessions? Since He is Lord, how are we to respond to His authority? Since He is our Savior and has taken God's wrath in our place, how are we to demonstrate our love and gratitude? *We must faithfully manage all that God has entrusted to us.*

The concept of management is illustrated in several ways in Scripture. One of the most familiar is the parable of the talents. (Note that a talent was not an ability, but a unit of money). Read this parable in Matthew 25:14-30 and discuss the following:

1. Complete the chart on the next page by discussing the three questions in the left column, applying them to each of the three slaves (managers). Write your observations in the appropriate columns:

2. What is the main point of this parable?

____

3. How does the parable represent our relationship to God?

____

____

4. What does God expect of us as His slave-managers? See Matthew 25:21; 1 Corinthians 4:1, 2?

____

____

	First Slave (Manager)	Second Slave (Manager)	Third Slave (Manager)
What was entrusted to him? (verses 14 and 15)			
What did he do with it? (verses 16-18)			
What was the result when the accounts were settled? (verses 19-30)			

Biblical Management

The principle of faithful management is illustrated by the life of Joseph (Genesis 39:2-6). Joseph's master, Potiphar, put Joseph in charge of his entire household. He entrusted to Joseph all that he had, and Joseph was responsible for managing His master's resources according to his master's priorities and desires.

Jesus taught that an important part of serving God is investing our resources (that is, the resources God has entrusted to us) in that which has eternal value. (See Matthew 6:19-24.) While this has obvious implications for giving money to support the work of God's kingdom, it also relates to the rest of our resources—what we do not put into the offering plate. We are to manage these resources according to God's values. We are not to allow these things to become our master; we are to use them to serve the Master.

The following chart summarizes some basic principles for the process of managing God's resources. Faithful managers will be constantly aware of this process and committed to it. Study the chart, look up the Scriptures, and then respond to the questions that follow the chart.

BIBLICAL MANAGEMENT

1. God owns everything (Deuteronomy 10:14)

2. God entrusts certain resources to us (Matthew 25:14)

3. We manage these resources according to God's purposes and desires (Matthew 6:33)

4. We will give an account for how effectively we have managed God's resources to accomplish His purposes (Matthew 25:19)

"Now it is required that those who have been given a trust [managers] must prove faithful" (1 Corinthians 4:2).

Questions to Consider

1. What on this chart makes the most sense to you? What is most unclear or creates the most questions?

____

____

2. How often are you conscious of any or all of these principles during an average day?

____

____

3. What most concerns you about these principles? What most excites you?

____

____

____

Managing God's Resources

All that God gives us is entrusted to us. He expects us to invest it in a way that will accomplish His purposes on earth. To squander it, use it selfishly, or bury it is unfaithful management. We will some day have to give account for how we use these resources. Even though we are saved by grace and not works, how we use these resources will have eternal consequences. To use them wisely and faithfully will result in rewards in Heaven. If we use them selfishly or unwisely, we will lose rewards when we get to Heaven (1 Corinthians 3:10-15).

Below are some of the resources God gives us. Consider at least one or two of them and study the related passages. Then answer this question, based upon the Scriptures listed (and others you might think of): *How does God expect us to manage this?* Jot your ideas in the appropriate column of the chart.

RESOURCE	HOW GOD EXPECTS US TO MANAGE IT
TIME/OPPORTUNITIES Ephesians 5:15-18 Colossians 4:5, 6 Galatians 6:10	
FAMILY Colossians 3:18-21 1 Timothy 3:4, 5, 12 Deuteronomy 6:4-9	
MONEY/POSSESSIONS Matthew 6:19-21 Luke 16:10-13 1 Timothy 6:17-19	

MIND/THOUGHTS Romans 12:2 Romans 8:5, 8 Ephesians 4:20-24	
BODY 1 Corinthians 6:19, 20 Romans 6:11-13 Philippians 1:20	
THE GOSPEL (TRUTH, SCRIPTURES) 1 Timothy 6:20, 21 2 Timothy 1:13, 14 2 Timothy 3:16, 17	
SPIRITUAL GIFTS 1 Peter 4:10, 11 Romans 12:4-8 1 Corinthians 12:4-7	
PHYSICAL SKILLS/ABILITIES Ecclesiastes 9:10 Colossians 3:17 Colossians 3:23	
WORK/EMPLOYMENT Ephesians 6:5-9 Colossians 3:22—4:1 Titus 2:9, 10	

Getting Personal

1. In what areas have you sought to be a faithful manager of God's possessions?

___

___

2. In what area will you seek to become a more faithful manager?

___

___

Scripture Memory Verse

1 Corinthians 4:2 or Luke 12:48b

For Further Reflection

Complete the resource chart under the section *Managing God's Resources* by looking up the Scriptures and answering the questions for those sections you did not complete today.

Counting Time or Making Time Count?

Managing God's Time

It's About Time

How do you view time? What are your major frustrations about time? Of what time-affected opportunities are you best at taking advantage? Follow the instructions below to evaluate your experience in time management.

1. Which of the time problems below do you find creeping into your life? Put a mark (✓) beside each one you consider to be a concern:

__ Too much time
__ Not enough time
__ Don't know where to begin in using my time
__ Don't know how to prioritize my time
__ Wasting time
__ Overcommitment of time
__ Lack of purpose in using my time
__ Always late for appointments and deadlines
__ Lack of adequate scheduling
__ Never know what day of the week it is
__ Lack of personal discipline
__ Too many people control my time
__ Little details eat up my time

2. Complete these sentences in your own words:

   a. My greatest frustration about time is … ________________________________ .

   ____

   b. The best advice I've heard about managing time is … ______________________ .

   ____

Time and Purpose

God is the owner of everything. That includes our time and our schedules. In response to God's ownership, His lordship, and His saving grace, our desire is to use our time in a way that pleases Him. The proper question is not, "What do I want to do with my time?" but, "What does God want me to do—with His time?" Obviously, the answer to both of these questions will often be the same. And the more like Christ we become, the more our natural desire will be God's desire. But faithful time management begins with asking the right question.

As God's servants, we are concerned about faithful, wise use of our time. Managing our schedules and the opportunities God gives us in an obedient, discerning way is commanded in Scripture. We are instructed to manage our time wisely, especially in two specific areas:

• **We need wisdom to distinguish between moral and immoral choices.**
Therefore be careful how you walk, *not as unwise men, but as wise, making the most of your time*, because the days are evil. So then do not be foolish, but understand what the will of the Lord is. And do not get drunk with wine, for that is dissipation, but be filled with the Spirit (Ephesians 5:15-18, NASB).

- **We need wisdom to use our opportunities for maximum results.**
  Conduct yourselves *with wisdom* toward outsiders, *making the most of the opportunity* (Colossians 4:5, NASB).

  So then, *while we have opportunity*, let us do good to all men, and especially to those who are of the household of the faith (Galatians 6:10, NASB).

We must discern and use the opportunities to influence unbelievers for Christ and to build up and encourage each other. To gain the wisdom to do this—the wisdom God expects of us—we must first learn what God desires most in our lives. Then we must order our lives and schedules accordingly. We must acknowledge God as the complete owner of our time and seek to invest it in His purposes.

Read the passages cited below and discuss this question: *What major purpose for my life is presented in this passage?* Write your insights in the space provided.

Matthew 6:33 ______________________________

____

Matthew 22:35-40 ______________________________

____

Matthew 28:18-20 ______________________________

____

1 Corinthians 10:31 ______________________________

____

Philippians 3:7-11 ______________________________

____

Time and Wisdom

To invest time effectively in God's purposes requires wisdom regarding three issues: (1) doing the right thing (2) in the right way (3) for the right reasons. These three concerns can be discerned by asking three questions:

A. *What* should I do?

B. *How* should I do it?

C. *Why* should I do it?

1. What Should I Do? (Doing the Right Things)

The best decisions are not always clear. Life is complex and often confusing. God has not promised to make our decisions easy to figure out. He has not installed a celestial fax machine to transmit clear step-by-step directions whenever we ask.

Of course, we can be sure of what He has put in His Word, the Bible. Sometimes Scripture speaks directly to our need, so the guidance is very specific. But outside of clear Scriptural command, we are in less certain territory. We often have to make decisions that we think are in response to God's leading, but we have no definite guarantee. That is where faith enters the picture. And through our faith, God sometimes teaches us more when we are confused about decisions than when we are certain.

God does guide. But how do we determine how we should use our time and make decisions in harmony with the way He is leading? The following questions, while not exhaustive, are offered to help you make a start in considering how God is guiding.

• *Do the Scriptures speak directly to this situation?*

Although the Bible is relevant for every situation, it does not always define exactly what we should do in a specific situation. Still, it is the foundation of our decision-making process. Many of our decisions are directly answered by Scripture: we are to live honestly and with integrity; we are not to seek revenge; we are to run from sexual temptations. These and many other clear instructions give us a framework in which to make decisions.

But what if the Bible does not address the issue you are facing—or does not give a complete answer? What if there are several options available, all of which are in harmony with God's revealed Word? How do you know which to choose? Another question needs to be asked.

• *What is the best option I can choose at this time?*

The best option is the one that will best glorify God, best build up others in the body, best influence others to God, and/or best draw you closer to God. The answer still may not be easy to determine, but these issues must not be ignored when facing a difficult decision.

Part of the process of maturing in Christ is learning to be able to discern between what is good and what is best. Paul prayed for this kind of wisdom for the Philippian Christians—that they would "be able to discern what is best" (Philippians 1:10).

2. **How Should I Do It? (Doing the Right Thing *in the Right Way*)**

The manner in which we do something has spiritual implications. Good, righteous actions done in sloppy or thoughtless ways may not have positive results. How can we be sure that we are operating in an effective manner? To answer that question, considering the following two questions may be helpful.

• *What is the most loving way I can do this?*

The two greatest commandments are to love God and to love others (Matthew 22:37-40). This gives high priority to seeking the most loving way to do *everything* that we do.

We need to cultivate the habit of thinking about the real needs of others if we want to manage God's time well. Otherwise, we might waste good opportunities by handling them in an insensitive way.

• *How can I do my best in this situation?*

Sloppiness is not a virtue. Halfheartedness brings no smiles in Heaven. Just because we are involved in good activities does not mean that God is pleased. The norm for the Christian is to seek excellence. God honors excellence because excellence honors God (when it is done in His name). Note Ecclesiastes 9:10; Colossians 3:17; 1 Corinthians 10:31.

3. **Why Should I Do It? (Doing the Right Things in the Right Way *for the Right Reasons*)**

   Our motives are just as important to God as our actions—perhaps more so. Jesus had strong condemnation for hypocrites who did religious activity just to impress others (Matthew 6:1-18; 23:1-7, 27, 28). Good deeds done for selfish reasons offend God and forfeit His blessing.

   But good activity done with the intent of pleasing and honoring God delights Him. Obedience that stems from gratitude to God and love for Him brings Him pleasure.

   In a very real sense, we might conclude that the best management of time occurs when God powerfully works in us to accomplish His priorities. Here are several questions to help us evaluate our motivation for how we manage God's time:

- *Will I do this out of love for God?*

  We can't do anything to make God love or accept us any more than He already does! He has lavished His grace upon you. Cherish that thought and let your love for Christ swell and burst inside of you as a result. Thank Him continuously for His incredible mercy. And then seek to express your love for Him by doing good works. Think of them as "thank-you notes."

- *Will I do this to exalt God?*

  Faithful time management results in God's getting maximum glory. As God's servants, we desire for God to receive the credit that is due Him. So God's faithful manager will do things with the desire that others will be impressed with God, not with God's manager.

- *Will I do it with the intent of advancing God's kingdom?*

  Seeking God's kingdom is of major concern for those who manage God's resources faithfully. Although it involves much more than this, it includes seeking to bring those who are outside His kingdom into the kingdom. In addition, it involves encouraging those who are in God's kingdom to live obediently to the King.

Applying the Three Principles

Sue knows her boss (Mrs. Jeffries) is under a lot of pressure to complete a project. Sue has also been working on the project and knows she is very competent to complete it by herself. She decides that she can help her boss by offering to do more than is required of her (*doing the right thing*). But she wants to help in a way that Mrs. Jeffries perceives as helpful, and without threatening her. So she sensitively asks if there is more she can do to help, being careful to ask in a supportive way (doing the right thing *in the right way*). Her motive is neither to impress Mrs. Jeffries or her co-workers, but to show the love of Christ. In addition, she hopes it will build a relationship with Mrs. Jeffries that will allow her someday to share her faith with her (doing the right thing in the right way *for the right reasons*).

Questions to Consider

1. What is an example of doing the right thing in the right way *for the wrong reasons*?

   ____

   ____

   ____

2. What is an example of doing the *wrong* thing for the *right* reasons?

3. What is an example of doing the *right* thing for the *right* reason in the *wrong* way?

Investing Time Wisely

The following is a chart to help you apply God's purposes to your major time commitments. In the cone are listed several *major purposes* in time management. (These purposes are suggested by the Scriptures you studied earlier.)

At the bottom of the cone are some *major areas* in which most Christians invest their time (other areas could have been included as well). Our purposes as we participate in these areas ought to be centered around the purposes suggested in the cone. On the following page, select two or three of these areas and respond to this question: *How can time in this area be managed in a way that fulfills our major purposes?* Jot your ideas on the chart. An example is provided in each area:

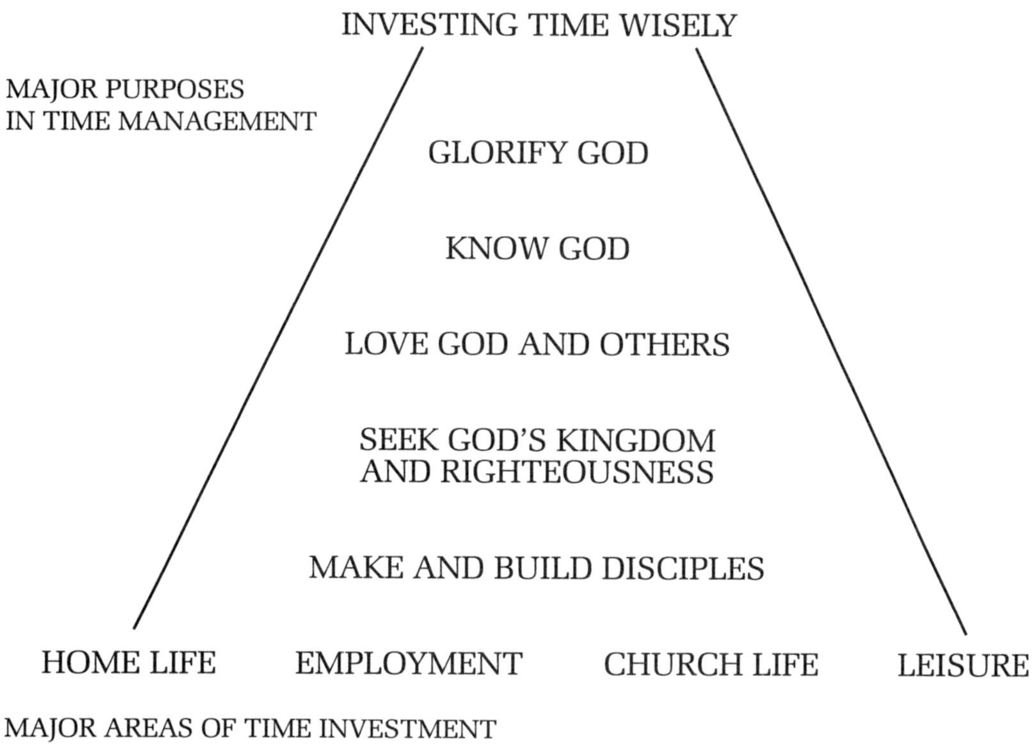

How can time in each area be managed in a way that fulfills our major purposes?

Area	How to Manage It According to God's Purposes
HOME LIFE (Relationships and Family Commitments)	Example: Focus on building loving relationships with each family member.
EMPLOYMENT (Work)	Example: Seek to make my employer successful by what I do.
CHURCH LIFE (Relationships and Commitments in Christ's Body)	Example: Participate regularly in a ministry that utilizes my spiritual gifts and meets others' needs.
LEISURE (Time to Use at Your Discretion)	Example: Use some of my leisure time to build relationships with neighbors who need to know Christ.

Time Pressure and You

Do you have enough time? If you're like most, you would answer no. But the truth is, there isn't any more. Few people have enough time, yet everyone has all there is. No one has more time than you do. But knowing that doesn't relieve the pressure we feel from a society that is progressing at a lightning pace. So what can we do to make the most of our time for God's sake? The following are suggestions for coping with time pressure:

- ***Give God Ownership of Each Day***

Start each day by acknowledging to God that it is His day and that you want to use it to please Him.

- ***Keep Your Priorities Clearly in Focus***

Write down what you think God's priorities are and keep these written priorities in a place you will likely see them often. Review these priorities throughout the day and plan your activities according to them.

- ***Strive for Balance Between Being God's Person and Doing God's Work***

Faithful time management requires us to focus on our character as well as our activities. Focusing exclusively on either our internal life or our external life is contrary to Christ's teaching and risks living an ineffective life.

- ***Reduce Your Expectations***

We have many options in life—more than we could ever do. Wisdom involves being realistic in assessing what we can and cannot do. Discernment realizes that we cannot do everything that interests us. It forces us to make hard choices between options, based on priorities and not on impulses.

• ***Turn Off the Television***

Television as a medium is morally neutral. The content determines its moral value. Many programs ought to be considered off limits for a Christian, but some are wholesome.

Even if all its programming were morally sound, however, television carries some major cautions. High on the list is that it can become addictive; it invites us to waste hour after hour gazing at the screen while we forfeit opportunities to do good.

A Christian who is committed to investing his or her time for God's glory will have to ask some hard questions about television—like, "How much time can I really afford to watch television, considering God's priorities for my life?" "What are more productive ways of investing my time?"

• ***Take Time to Relax and Enjoy Life***

Productivity ought not to be defined only in terms of activity and accomplishment. The quality of our character and the degree of our personal relationship with God are essential aspects of our productivity, and neither can be measured or defined in terms of visible accomplishment.

If we do not include regular periods for relaxing and resting and enjoying life, we will risk burnout. Sometimes the most spiritual thing we can do is rest. (Of course, it is possible to focus too much on rest and recreation, or falsely to define it exclusively in terms of entertainment, which is not necessarily equivalent to rest.)

• ***Resist Becoming a Slave to the Urgent Demands of Life***

Charles Hummel's classic booklet, *The Tyranny of the Urgent*, emphasizes a distinction between what is urgent and what is important. The urgent are those things that demand immediate action. Frequently, they do not contribute to the Christian's highest priorities. The important things are those that are of high priority in terms of one's whole life. The important things are usually long-term; they rarely scream for our attention.

We can live our entire lives responding to one urgency after another, and allow them to crowd out those important involvements that have no deadlines. But in the long run, we will pay for neglecting our high priorities. Our lives will drift toward shallowness.

Memory Verse

Matthew 6:33 or Ephesians 5:15, 16

For Further Reflection

To expand your application of today's study, complete the chart on page 40. This is an important (though not necessarily urgent) part of this study. Even if there isn't time to complete it in your initial study time, be sure you return to it and finish it.

Think about the following two questions and write your conclusions on the chart below. (One example is given in each column for each area.)

1. In what ways am I presently managing this area according to God's purposes?

2. What is one thing I can do differently to manage this area better according to God's purposes?

Area	What Am I Presently Doing?	How Can I Better Manage?
HOME LIFE	EXAMPLE: Attending kids' sports events.	EXAMPLE: Focus dinner conversations on other family members.
EMPLOYMENT	EXAMPLE: Trying not to waste time, but still not getting enough done.	EXAMPLE: Set realistic goals and prioritize my daily plans by them.
CHURCH LIFE	EXAMPLE: Meeting with a small group for Bible study and prayer.	EXAMPLE: Invite other church members home for a meal on a regular basis.
LEISURE	EXAMPLE: Walking 30 minutes per day.	EXAMPLE: Limit television viewing to four hours per week.

Investing in Eternity
Managing God's Money

The Pros and Cons of Money

Money has many advantages. Few people would disagree with that comment. But it also has many dangers. Think about the following two questions, and list as many ideas as you can in the space below.

1. What are benefits of money?

2. What are dangers and disadvantages of money?

Benefits	***Dangers/Disadvantages***
____________________	____________________
____________________	____________________
____________________	____________________
____________________	____________________

God's Perspective of Money

A significant implication of God's ownership is that all of our money actually belongs to Him. He has entrusted it to us so that we may invest it in a way that accomplishes His desires. We are to manage God's money faithfully and wisely. This is not seen in Scripture as a matter of drudgery, but a privilege. The God who created us and saved us commands us to use His money according to His purposes. Having received His grace, our response of love should lead us to seek to please Him in this area.

Just as faithful management of God's time begins with asking the right question, so does proper management of the money He has entrusted to us. The question is not, "What do I want to do with my money?" It is, "What does God want me to do with His money?"

1. Read Matthew 6:19-24 and answer these related questions:

   a. Why are treasures invested in Heaven superior to treasures invested on earth (vs. 19, 20)?

   ____

   b. What are spiritual consequences of investing our treasures on earth (v. 21)?

   ____

   c. What are spiritual results of investing our treasures in Heaven (v. 24)?

   ____

d. Why can't we serve both God and money (v. 24)?

____

2. According to the following verses, what should be our attitude toward money?

Psalm 62:10b _______________

____

Hebrews 13:5 _______________

____

1 Timothy 6:6-10 _______________

____

3. According to these verses, what are high priorities for using God's money?

Proverbs 3:9, 10 _______________

____

Matthew 10:8 _______________

____

Malachi 3:10 _______________

____

1 Timothy 5:8 _______________

____

Acts 20:35 _______________

____

4. How can we know that we are investing our treasure in Heaven and not on earth?

____

____

When we accept our role as *managers* of God's money, we are free to focus on investing it in eternal things. Although we have great freedom in specific choices, our Lord's priorities cause us to reject self-indulgence. Accumulation of wealth as a primary goal is seen as foolishness. Why would we want to waste our lives stockpiling something that is, so to speak, disintegrating? While wealth is not essentially evil, when we take our role as managers seriously, we are not deceived by the fleetingness of money. We seek to lay up treasures in Heaven, not on earth.

Investing God's money (treasures) in eternal things has some practical implications. It means that we seek to use money in a way that will honor God, fulfill our responsibilities, and meet the needs of others. Included in this are such uses as providing for our families (and our own basic living), giving to the Lord's church, and giving to help the poor and needy. While this list is not exhaustive, it does suggest several high priorities for the investment of money.

The wise and faithful manager refuses to become addicted to money. He neither sets his heart on it nor trusts in it. He is free to use it, even to enjoy it (1 Timothy 6:17-19) . . . but not to love it. His passion is for God, not riches.

Purposes of Christian Giving

In what ways can we give to God? How can we honor Him with our money (Proverbs 3:9, 10)? What should the money be used to accomplish when we give it? Consider two main ways of giving to God. The ultimate goal of both ways is to glorify God, and each giving carries an additional purpose with it. Both of these are commanded by God and are not options. We cannot choose one and ignore the other.

- *We give to support the ministry of Christ's church and the advancement of the gospel* (1 Corinthians 9:1-12; 1 Timothy 5:17, 18; Galatians 6:6; Luke 10:7).

  In the Old Testament, tithes (10% of a person's total income) were required. These were given to God through the priests and were used to support the temple ministry. (Specifically it was given to the Levites—the priestly tribe—who ministered in God's service. See Deuteronomy 14:27-29.)

  Because every Old Testament believer received from the temple ministry, each one was required to support it with tithes. In addition to tithes, these believers gave a variety of special offerings to God for various purposes. (The burnt offering, grain offering, fellowship offering, sin offering, and guilt offering are prescribed in Leviticus 1-7.) These offerings were to be given in gratitude and reverence.

  In the New Testament, we see a similar pattern. Every believer is commanded to give generously to support the church he receives from and participates in. This is a clear carry-over from Old Testament principles (see the New Testament passages above). Although the Old Testament believer gave tithes for this purpose, no such percentage is given in the New Testament. The principle is generosity. And generosity must be seen at least in terms of Old Testament standards—certainly not less than them. If the Old Testament believer could give a tithe even though he didn't have a full understanding of grace, we who know of Christ's sacrifice should desire to give at least as much.

- *We give to assist the poor and needy* (Romans 15:26; 1 Corinthians 16:1-4; 2 Corinthians 8:1-5; 9:12; James 1:27; 2:14-17; 1 John 3:16-18).

  God has always had compassion on the poor. Jesus' ministry emphasized helping the poor (Luke 4:18; Matthew 11:5; 19:21; Luke 12:33), and Christians are commanded to give to the poor (passages cited above). No set amount is suggested; once again, generosity is the rule. If we have received the love of Christ and do not show it to others in need, we are living a contradiction.

What About the Rest?

Managing God's money means that we are concerned not only about what we give, but also about what we do with the rest of God's money. We are to manage it wisely, in a godly and nonwasteful manner. What we do with the rest of God's money (what we don't give in offerings) is a part of management. Decisions about spending and saving and investing are just as spiritually important as decisions about giving.

How can we manage the rest of God's money in wise, God-pleasing ways? Think about that and list below some *dos* and *don'ts* for managing the rest of God's money. A few examples are provided to generate your thinking.

DOs	DON'Ts
Have a budget and follow it as a guideline	Don't focus on acquiring great wealth
______________________	______________________
______________________	______________________
______________________	______________________
______________________	______________________

Applying the Truth

How can we move from looking at truth to living the truth? Discuss these questions with that goal in mind:

1. What tends to keep Christians from seeing their money as God's money?

____

____

2. How can we help each other remember that our money belongs to God?

____

____

3. What are ways we can free up more money to give to God's kingdom and His purposes?

____

____

Memory Verse

Matthew 6:21 or Proverbs 3:9

Session Guide for Leaders

Lesson One

Central Truth

Because God is Creator and Owner of the universe, we must yield to Him ownership of our lives—all we are and have.

Learning Goals

By the end of this session, the students will do the following:

1. *Conclude* that God owns their lives and possessions.
2. *Explore* specific implications of God's ownership.
3. *Evaluate* how consistently they have yielded ownership of their lives to God.

Session Strategy

Preparation

Have the students complete the instructions under *This Land Is Whose Land?* Allow seven to ten minutes for this section.

Exploration

Read the introductory paragraph under *Getting Back to Basics.* Then have the class form at least two groups. (If you have more than sixteen students, form more groups, and have more than one group work on the same assignment.) Assign four of the Bible passages to each group, and instruct the group to assign a discussion leader. Have the rest of the group members take notes, and give the groups twelve to fifteen minutes to complete the assignment. When time has expired, ask each group leader to read the summary statements.

Read the paragraphs following the list of Scriptures. Then have the students discuss the four questions following the paragraphs in their small groups. (If your time is limited, these questions can be omitted.)

Application

1. Direct the students to the section entitled *Listing God's Assets.* Lead the students in brainstorming the two questions. This can be done as a large group or in small groups. Allow no more than ten minutes for this part of the lesson.

2. Have the students complete the directions under *What's Your Opinion?* Allow two or three minutes for students to identify their opinions and mark the appropriate column for each statement. Then take a tally for each statement. Ask those who marked SA to raise their hands, then those who marked MA, then those who checked MD, finally those who marked SD. If there is a significant difference of opinion on any of them, ask someone from the minority group to defend that position. Allow brief discussion from both sides. As teacher, your role in an Agree/Disagree activity is to remain neutral and encourage the students to discuss what they honestly think.

Option: If you prefer, you can omit the two previous steps and lead the class through the section, *Living Under God's Ownership.* Do this as a whole class or in small groups, reading the paragraphs and then discussing the related questions.

3. Read the paragraphs under *Getting Personal.* Then have the students mark the continuum according to the instructions. Afterward, ask them to jot down their answers to the questions that follow the continuum.

Continuation

This part of the lesson is to be completed at home (and can be shared with a spouse, friend, or discussed at the beginning of class the following week). Before dismissing class in prayer, direct the students' attention to the section *For Further Reflection.* Explain the activity and recommend that students complete it later that day or during the week and discuss it with another person. Encourage them to bring it back to class the next week *if* you intend to make time for it the next lesson.

Lesson Two

Central Truth

Because Jesus is Lord, we owe Him total submission and obedience.

Learning Goals

By the end of this session, the students will do the following:

1. *Explain* that, because Jesus is Lord, we are to live in obedience to Him.
2. *Identify* a personal response to Jesus as Lord.
3. *Determine* to develop a life of submission to Jesus.

Session Strategy

Preparation

Direct the students' attention to the *Getting Started* section. Read statements A and B. Then lead a discussion of the two related questions.

Exploration

1. Continue by reading the introductory paragraphs under *Lordship and Obedience*. Then have the students form two or three groups. (Each group should have at least four people.) Assign each discussion group a set of passages listed in the *Convince Me!* section. They are to follow the directions given in the paragraph preceding the list of Scriptures.

2. After about fifteen minutes, bring the groups back together as a class. Ask the group leaders to summarize the groups' observations.

3. Read the *Lord and Savior* section, and move on to the section entitled *Jesus Is Lord: Overview*. Have the students read that on their own and fill in the blanks on the outline. The following is suggested to assist students who need help on the outline:

Jesus Is Lord

A. In Creation (Colossians 1:15-18)
B. In Resurrection (Philippians 2:5-11)
C. In Judgment (Romans 14:7-12; 2 Corinthians 5:9, 10)
D. In Our Lives (Colossians 3:17)

Discuss this briefly and move on to step 4.

4. Read the introductory paragraph under *The Meaning of Lordship*. Then read the excerpt from *Call to Discipleship* by Juan Carlos Ortz. Afterward, have the students discuss the questions under *Your Reaction*.

Application

1. Direct the students to the section entitled *Jesus Is Lord: So What?* Read the paragraphs and have the students discuss the related questions. These may be discussed in the large group or in small groups.

2. Continue to the section entitled *Responding to Jesus as Lord*. Read the introductory paragraphs and have the students complete the two sentences.

Option. If time is limited, choose 1 or 2 above.

Continuation

Encourage the students to continue this study during the week by completing the study under *For Further Reflection*.

Lesson Three

Central Truth

As our Savior, Jesus has saved us from God's wrath and has given us eternal life.

Learning Goals

By the end of this session, the students will do the following:

1. *Summarize* the message of salvation.
2. *Explain* that the appropriate response to Jesus as Savior is to live a life of good works.

Session Strategy

Preparation

Have the students focus on the section entitled *So Great a Salvation*. Read the introductory paragraphs. Then have students follow the instructions. Allow two or three minutes for the students to complete the activities. Ask them to share with others in small groups some of their observations for the three instructions.

Exploration

1. Direct the students to the section, *We Need A Savior.* After reading the opening paragraphs, have the students complete the study of Titus 3:3-8 and Ephesians 2:1-10 in the same small groups they-formed earlier.

Option: If time is limited, assign each passage to half the groups and allow the groups to report to the class what they learned.

2. To summarize your study of Ephesians 2 and Titus 3, read the section *Salvation in a Nutshell*. Discuss the similarities between this section and the students' own discoveries.

3. Students are to discuss the four questions under *Summarizing the Gospel*.

Application

1. Guide the students through the section entitled *Jesus is Savior: So What?* Read the paragraphs and discuss the related questions. (Using small groups will likely enhance the discussion here.)

2. After reading the beginning paragraph under *My Prayer of Gratitude*, ask students to complete the written prayer in their own words. If you have time, you might ask volunteers to share their prayers in a prayer time.

Continuation

Have the students read the directions under *For Further Reflection* and encourage them to complete the page entitled *My Ephesians 2 Testimony.*

Lesson Four

Central Truth

We are God's servants entrusted with His resources to manage according to His purposes.

Learning Goals

By the end of this session, the students will do the following:

1. *Identify* their relationship to God as that of managers to an owner.
2. *Determine* how they are to manage specific resources God has entrusted to them.

Session Strategy

Preparation

Have the students work in small groups of four to six people to complete the chart under *Entrusting Your Resources to Others.* Allow three to five minutes for completion. Then ask each group to report their ideas for one or two of the items. Help them see that, in everyday life, we operate under a system of entrusting resources to others. And just as we expect faithful management of what we entrust to others, God expects faithful management of His resources entrusted to us.

Exploration

1. Direct the students' attention to the section entitled *A Parable.* Read the opening paragraphs and then have the students discuss the questions in their small groups. Give the students fifteen minutes to complete the discussion. Then ask the groups to summarize their conclusions for questions 2 and 3 for the rest of the class.

2. Continue to the section entitled *Biblical Management.* Read the paragraphs and the chart. Then lead the students in a discussion of the questions that follow the chart.

Application

1. Read the opening paragraphs under *Managing God's Resources.* Then have the students continue working in their small groups. Assign one or two of the items in the "Resource" column to each group. (Unless you have a large class, you won't have all the items assigned. That's okay.) Students are to follow the instructions. Allow each group up to ten minutes to complete the assignment. Then ask each group to give a brief summary of its conclusions for the rest of the class. Encourage the students to jot down the summaries from the other groups.

2. Have the students individually complete the section entitled *Getting Personal.* Allow several minutes. Then close with prayer.

Continuation

Encourage students to complete the instructions under *For Further Reflection* before the next session.

Lesson Five

Central Truth

God expects us to manage the time He has entrusted to us according to His purposes.

Learning Goals

By the end of this session, the students will do the following:

1. *Identify* major purposes God has for the time He has entrusted to them.
2. *Explore* ways they can faithfully manage areas of time investment.

Session Strategy

Preparation

Have the students complete the directions under the section, *It's About Time.* Allow three to five minutes for completion. Then ask the students to share their sentence completions in small groups. Allow about five minutes for these discussions.

Exploration

Read the paragraphs at the beginning of the section, *Time and Purpose.* Then have the students discuss the question and study the passages in the same groups they formed earlier. Allow ten or twelve minutes for exploring the Scriptures. Then ask groups for a quick summary of their observations.

Application

1. Read the section, *Time and Wisdom.*

2. Continue to the section, *Applying the Three Principles.* Read the example cited and have the students discuss the questions that follow.

3. Read the section, *Investing Time Wisely.* Then have the students work again in their small groups and assign each group one of the major areas of time investment listed on the chart. Then have them discuss the related question as it applies to their assigned area. Allow ten minutes for discussion. Then ask each group to report their ideas to the class.

4. Read the section, *Time and Pressure and You.* Then have the students consider this question: "As you consider these seven suggestions, which one do you think you need to concentrate on the most?" Discuss this issue together.

Option: If time is limited, omit either step 3 or 4 above. It may be recommended for the students to complete on their own outside of class.

Continuation

Explain the chart under *For Further Reflection,* emphasizing that it is the personal application of today's study. Encourage them to set aside some time early in the week to complete the chart and thus personalize the lesson.

Lesson Six

Central Truth

As faithful managers of God's money, we must seek to invest it according to God's desires, not our own.

Learning Goals

By the end of this session, the students will do the following:

1. *Pinpoint* God's priorities for investing His money.
2. *Determine* guidelines for managing the portion of God's money we keep.

Preparation

Lead the class in a brainstorm using the questions under *The Pros and Cons of Money.*

Exploration

1. Read the paragraphs under *God's Perspective of Money*. Then have the students complete the related assignments in small groups. Allow thirty minutes; then ask for a brief summary of question 4 from each group. After each group has presented its summary, read the paragraphs that follow the questions.
2. Read the section *Purposes of Christian Giving.*

Application

Have the students zero in on the section entitled *What About the Rest?* Read the paragraph and lead students in a brainstorm of *dos* and *don'ts* for managing the portion of God's money that we don't give away. Then have the students discuss the questions under *Applying the Truth.*